Rooted Connections Cultivating an Organic Family Legacy

S.K Jone

	Page No
Introduction	3
Chapter 1: The Power of Family Bonds	4
Chapter 2: Nurturing Core Values	6
Chapter 3: Growing Together: Communication and Connection	8
Chapter 4: Love and Respect: The Foundation of a Strong Family	10
Chapter 5: Embracing Traditions: Anchoring Your Legacy	12
Chapter 6: Creating Meaningful Memories	14
Chapter 7: Embracing Personal Growth and Individuality	16
Chapter 8: Adaptability and Resilience: Thriving Through Change	18
Chapter 9: Making a Difference: Giving Back as a Family	20
Chapter 10: Overcoming Challenges Together	22
Chapter 11: Healing and Forgiveness: Restoring Family Bonds	24
Chapter 12: Passing on the Torch: Ensuring a Lasting Legacy	26

Introduction

In the fast-paced and ever-changing world we live in, families often find themselves seeking stability, connection, and a sense of purpose. Rooted Connections: Cultivating an Organic Family Legacy is a book that delves into the art of intentionally building a family legacy that transcends generations. This book is a guide for families who aspire to create a lasting impact and cultivate deep-rooted connections within their family unit.

In our modern society, where technology and external distractions often take precedence, it becomes increasingly important to pause, reflect, and nurture the bonds that tie families together. Rooted Connections offers a roadmap for families to explore and discover their unique values, traditions, and shared experiences that shape their collective identity.

The concept of an organic family legacy highlights the significance of a naturally grown and authentic approach to family life. It emphasizes the idea that a legacy is not solely about material wealth or achievements, but rather about the intangible qualities that are passed down through generations: love, wisdom, values, and a sense of belonging. It is about fostering meaningful connections, nurturing growth, and leaving a positive imprint on the world through the collective actions of the family unit.

This book is divided into chapters that address various aspects of cultivating an organic family legacy. Each chapter offers insights, practical advice, and actionable steps to empower families to navigate the challenges, seize the opportunities, and deepen their connections. From nurturing core values to embracing traditions, from creating meaningful memories to overcoming challenges together, Rooted Connections explores the essential elements that contribute to a thriving family legacy.

Drawing upon research, personal anecdotes, and wisdom passed down through generations, Rooted Connections serves as a companion for families seeking to foster a strong and resilient bond. It is a call to prioritize family relationships, celebrate the uniqueness of each member, and cultivate a shared purpose that transcends individual achievements.

As you embark on this journey of cultivating an organic family legacy, remember that it is a continuous process that requires commitment, open communication, and a willingness to adapt. By embracing the principles and practices outlined in this book, you have the opportunity to lay the foundation for a legacy that will endure for years to come, anchoring your family in love, resilience, and a sense of belonging.

So, let us embark together on this transformative exploration of Rooted Connections, where we will uncover the beauty and power of cultivating an organic family legacy that will shape the lives of your loved ones for generations to come.

Chapter 1: The Power of Family Bonds

Exploring the unique and profound influence of family bonds on our lives.

Sharing personal anecdotes and research studies to highlight the significance of strong family connections.

Setting the stage for the exploration of the various aspects of family bonds and their impact on individual and collective well-being.

Section 1: The Essence of Family Bonds

Defining family bonds and their role in shaping our identities and sense of belonging.

Examining the emotional and psychological benefits of strong family connections, such as increased happiness, resilience, and improved mental health.

Exploring the evolutionary and biological roots of family bonds and their impact on human development.

Section 2: Nurturing Family Bonds

Discussing the importance of investing time, effort, and intentionality in nurturing family connections.

Exploring practical strategies for building and strengthening family bonds, such as regular family activities, shared experiences, and open communication.

Highlighting the significance of quality time, active listening, and empathy in fostering deeper connections within the family unit.

Section 3: Family Bonds and Personal Growth

Examining how family bonds contribute to individual growth, self-esteem, and personal development.

Discussing the role of family support in shaping values, aspirations, and career choices.

Exploring the influence of intergenerational bonds and the wisdom passed down through generations.

Section 4: The Resilience of Family Bonds

Discussing the role of family bonds in times of adversity, such as illness, loss, or challenging life transitions.

Sharing stories of families who have overcome challenges together and found strength in their bonds.

Highlighting the importance of support, understanding, and resilience-building within the family unit.

Section 5: Cultural and Legacy Connections

Exploring how family bonds contribute to cultural identity and heritage preservation.

Discussing the significance of family rituals, traditions, and celebrations in strengthening family bonds and passing down cultural values.

Highlighting the role of family history and storytelling in creating a sense of continuity and legacy.

Conclusion:

Summarizing the key insights and takeaways from the chapter.

Emphasizing the transformative power of family bonds and their impact on individual well-being and collective happiness.

Inspiring readers to prioritize and invest in nurturing their family connections, creating a strong foundation for a noble family legacy.

Chapter 2: Nurturing Core Values

Establishing the significance of core values in shaping a family's identity and character.

Exploring how core values provide a moral compass and guide decision-making within the family unit.

Setting the stage for an exploration of strategies to identify and nurture core values within the family.

Section 1: Identifying Family Core Values

Encouraging self-reflection and family discussions to identify the core values that resonate with each family member.

Providing guidance on exploring personal beliefs, principles, and priorities that form the foundation of family values.

Highlighting the importance of aligning individual values with shared family values to promote unity and cohesion.

Section 2: Instilling Core Values in Daily Life

Discussing practical ways to integrate core values into daily family routines and activities.

Exploring the role of modeling and leading by example in reinforcing core values.

Providing actionable strategies to create a values-based environment at home, such as establishing family rituals, setting clear expectations, and reinforcing positive behavior.

Section 3: Communicating and Reinforcing Core Values

Emphasizing the significance of open and honest communication in nurturing core values within the family.

Exploring effective ways to discuss and explain the rationale behind core values to children and teenagers.

Discussing the importance of reinforcing core values through consistent feedback, positive reinforcement, and constructive discipline.

Section 4: Resolving Conflicts and Decision-Making Based on Core Values

Discussing how core values can guide conflict resolution within the family.

Providing strategies for resolving conflicts that align with family values, such as active listening, empathy, and compromise.

Exploring how core values can inform decision-making processes, fostering integrity, and ethical choices.

Section 5: Flexibility and Adaptability in Core Values

Discussing the importance of flexibility and adaptability in allowing core values to evolve with changing times and circumstances.

Exploring how families can navigate differences in values and embrace diversity while still maintaining a strong foundation of shared core values.

Encouraging open-mindedness, respectful dialogue, and the willingness to learn from differing perspectives.

Conclusion:

Summarizing the key insights and takeaways from the chapter.

Emphasizing the transformative power of nurturing core values within the family.

Inspiring readers to engage in ongoing conversations and activities that reinforce core values, fostering a strong moral foundation and a noble family legacy.

Regenerate response

Chapter 3: Growing Together: Communication and Connection

Acknowledging the crucial role of effective communication and genuine connection in nurturing a strong family bond.

Exploring the ways in which open and meaningful communication can foster understanding, trust, and support within the family.

Setting the stage for an exploration of communication styles, techniques, and strategies for cultivating deeper connections.

Section 1: Understanding Communication Styles

Introducing different communication styles and their impact on family dynamics.

Exploring assertive, passive, and aggressive communication patterns and their consequences.

Encouraging self-awareness and reflection to identify individual communication styles within the family.

Section 2: Active Listening and Empathy

Highlighting the importance of active listening as a foundational skill for effective communication.

Providing practical tips and exercises to enhance active listening skills within the family.

Discussing the role of empathy in fostering understanding and compassion, promoting deeper connections.

Section 3: Expressing Emotions and Needs

Encouraging family members to express emotions and needs in a healthy and constructive manner.

Discussing the importance of creating a safe space for open communication and vulnerability within the family.

Offering guidance on expressing emotions assertively, while respecting others' boundaries and perspectives.

Section 4: Conflict Resolution and Problem-Solving

Exploring strategies for resolving conflicts and disagreements within the family.

Discussing the importance of effective communication in finding mutually beneficial solutions.

Introducing problem-solving techniques, such as active brainstorming and compromise, to strengthen family relationships.

Section 5: Fostering Connection through Quality Time

Highlighting the significance of dedicating quality time for meaningful family interactions.

Discussing the benefits of shared activities, family meals, and regular family outings.

Providing suggestions for creating traditions and rituals that promote bonding and connection.

Section 6: Technology and Communication

Addressing the impact of technology on family communication and connection.

Discussing strategies for balancing screen time and promoting face-to-face interactions.

Encouraging digital boundaries and fostering technology-free spaces to enhance family connections.

Conclusion:

Summarizing the key insights and takeaways from the chapter.

Emphasizing the transformative power of effective communication and genuine connection within the family.

Inspiring readers to prioritize active listening, empathy, and quality time to cultivate stronger bonds and a nurturing family environment.

Chapter 4: Love and Respect: The Foundation of a Strong Family

Highlighting the fundamental importance of love and respect in nurturing a strong and harmonious family.

Exploring how love and respect form the bedrock of healthy relationships and contribute to a positive family dynamic.

Setting the stage for an exploration of practical strategies to cultivate love and respect within the family.

Section 1: Understanding Love and Respect

Defining love and respect within the context of family relationships.

Exploring the interconnected nature of love and respect and their impact on family well-being.

Discussing the significance of unconditional love and genuine respect as cornerstones of a strong family foundation.

Section 2: Expressing Love and Affection

Discussing different love languages and how they can be expressed within the family.

Exploring practical ways to show love and affection, such as through verbal affirmations, acts of kindness, and physical touch.

Emphasizing the importance of consistent expressions of love to strengthen family bonds.

Section 3: Cultivating Respect and Empathy

Highlighting the importance of respect as a core value within the family.

Discussing strategies for fostering respect, such as active listening, valuing differing opinions, and practicing empathy.

Exploring the role of boundaries and mutual understanding in promoting respectful interactions.

Section 4: Conflict Resolution with Love and Respect

Discussing the role of love and respect in conflict resolution within the family.

Providing practical strategies for resolving conflicts with empathy and open communication.

Emphasizing the importance of maintaining love and respect even during challenging times.

Section 5: Strengthening Emotional Connections

Exploring ways to strengthen emotional connections within the family.

Discussing the importance of emotional support, validation, and active engagement in family members' lives.

Introducing activities and rituals that promote emotional bonding and connection.

Section 6: Modeling Love and Respect

Discussing the influential role of parental modeling in fostering love and respect within the family.

Emphasizing the importance of setting positive examples through actions, words, and attitudes.

Encouraging parents and caregivers to cultivate self-awareness and practice self-care to model love and respect effectively.

Conclusion:

Summarizing the key insights and takeaways from the chapter.

Emphasizing the transformative power of love and respect in building a strong family foundation.

Inspiring readers to prioritize love and respect as foundational values within their own families, fostering a nurturing and harmonious environment for all members.

Chapter 5: Embracing Traditions: Anchoring Your Legacy

Recognizing the significance of traditions in preserving family identity and anchoring a lasting legacy.

Exploring how traditions create a sense of belonging, continuity, and connection across generations.

Setting the stage for an exploration of the importance of embracing traditions and practical strategies for incorporating them into family life.

Section 1: Understanding the Role of Traditions

Defining traditions and their role in family dynamics and cultural heritage.

Exploring the emotional and psychological benefits of traditions, such as fostering a sense of belonging and providing stability.

Discussing how traditions contribute to the transmission of values, beliefs, and customs.

Section 2: Identifying and Creating Meaningful Traditions

Encouraging reflection and family discussions to identify existing traditions and their significance.

Discussing the importance of creating new traditions that reflect the values and interests of the family.

Providing guidance on incorporating elements from different cultural backgrounds to create a rich tapestry of traditions.

Section 3: Celebrating Milestones and Festivities

Discussing the role of traditions in commemorating significant life events and holidays.

Exploring ways to infuse meaning and purpose into celebrations, ensuring they reflect family values and promote togetherness.

Providing suggestions for incorporating rituals, symbolic gestures, and storytelling into milestone celebrations.

Section 4: Passing Down Family Stories and Wisdom

Emphasizing the importance of storytelling in preserving family history and wisdom.

Discussing strategies for capturing and sharing family stories, ensuring they are passed down through generations.

Exploring the role of oral traditions, photo albums, journals, and digital platforms in documenting and sharing family narratives.

Section 5: Nurturing Cultural Heritage

Exploring ways to embrace and celebrate cultural heritage within the family.

Discussing the importance of learning about ancestral traditions, languages, and customs.

Encouraging participation in cultural events, festivals, and community activities to foster a connection to cultural roots.

Section 6: Evolving Traditions for the Modern Family

Acknowledging the need for adaptability and evolution of traditions to suit the changing needs and dynamics of the modern family.

Discussing ways to incorporate innovation and flexibility into existing traditions without compromising their core essence.

Emphasizing the importance of maintaining the spirit of tradition while embracing the realities of contemporary life.

Conclusion:

Summarizing the key insights and takeaways from the chapter.

Emphasizing the transformative power of embracing traditions in preserving family identity and anchoring a lasting legacy.

Inspiring readers to actively incorporate meaningful traditions into their family life, nurturing a sense of continuity, connection, and a noble family legacy.

Chapter 6: Creating Meaningful Memories

Recognizing the importance of creating lasting memories within the family.

Exploring how meaningful memories contribute to emotional connections, happiness, and the fabric of family identity.

Setting the stage for an exploration of practical strategies to create and cherish meaningful memories together.

Section 1: The Significance of Meaningful Memories

Discussing the impact of meaningful memories on family relationships and well-being.

Exploring how shared experiences and memories create a sense of unity and belonging.

Highlighting the long-term benefits of positive memories for individual and family resilience.

Section 2: Building Traditions of Memory Making

Discussing the role of traditions in creating a framework for meaningful memory making.

Providing guidance on establishing regular family rituals and traditions that foster memorable moments.

Encouraging creativity and flexibility in adapting traditions to fit the unique needs and interests of the family.

Section 3: Embracing Spontaneity and Adventure

Encouraging families to embrace spontaneity and seize opportunities for adventure and exploration.

Discussing the benefits of stepping out of routines and comfort zones to create extraordinary memories.

Providing practical suggestions for incorporating elements of surprise and adventure into everyday life.

Section 4: Capturing and Preserving Memories

Discussing the importance of capturing and preserving memories for posterity.

Exploring various methods of documenting memories, such as photographs, journals, scrapbooks, and digital platforms.

Providing practical tips on organizing and storing memories to ensure they are easily accessible and cherished over time.

Section 5: Creating Meaningful Family Traditions

Discussing the role of family traditions in fostering meaningful memories.

Providing examples of traditions that promote connection, laughter, and joy within the family.

Encouraging families to actively engage in the creation and continuation of traditions that hold special meaning to them.

Section 6: Mindful Presence and Quality Time

Emphasizing the importance of being fully present and engaged in creating meaningful memories.

Discussing the benefits of quality time spent together, free from distractions and technology.

Providing practical suggestions for fostering mindful presence and deep connection during shared experiences.

Conclusion:

Summarizing the key insights and takeaways from the chapter.

Emphasizing the transformative power of creating and cherishing meaningful memories within the family.

Inspiring readers to prioritize and invest in memory making, fostering a tapestry of beautiful moments that contribute to a rich and cherished family legacy.

Chapter 7: Embracing Personal Growth and Individuality

Recognizing the importance of personal growth and individuality within the family unit.

Exploring how embracing personal growth contributes to the overall well-being and harmony of the family.

Setting the stage for an exploration of strategies to support individuality while fostering a strong family bond.

Section 1: Nurturing Personal Development

Discussing the significance of personal growth and development within the family context.

Encouraging family members to identify their unique strengths, talents, and passions.

Providing guidance on setting personal goals and cultivating a growth mindset.

Section 2: Supporting Individuality within the Family

Discussing the importance of embracing and celebrating each family member's individuality.

Exploring ways to support and respect individual interests, hobbies, and aspirations.

Encouraging open communication and understanding to foster an environment where everyone's individuality is valued.

Section 3: Encouraging Autonomy and Independence

Discussing the importance of fostering autonomy and independence within the family.

Exploring age-appropriate opportunities for decision-making and responsibility.

Providing guidance on striking a balance between autonomy and familial support.

Section 4: Cultivating a Culture of Learning and Curiosity

Emphasizing the value of lifelong learning and curiosity within the family.

Discussing ways to create a culture of intellectual growth and exploration.

Encouraging family members to engage in shared learning experiences and intellectual discussions.

Section 5: Supporting Personal Goals and Aspirations

Discussing strategies for supporting individual goals and aspirations within the family.

Emphasizing the importance of encouragement, belief, and practical assistance.

Providing suggestions for creating a supportive environment that nurtures personal growth.

Section 6: Respecting Differences and Navigating Conflicts

Discussing the significance of respecting and embracing differences within the family.

Providing strategies for navigating conflicts that arise due to individuality and differing opinions.

Emphasizing the importance of empathy, active listening, and compromise in resolving conflicts constructively.

Conclusion:

Summarizing the key insights and takeaways from the chapter.

Emphasizing the transformative power of embracing personal growth and individuality within the family.

Inspiring readers to create an environment that supports and celebrates each family member's journey of personal development, fostering a strong family bond while honoring individuality.

Chapter 8: Adaptability and Resilience: Thriving Through Change

Recognizing the inevitability of change and the importance of adaptability and resilience within the family.

Exploring how embracing change and developing resilience can strengthen family bonds and promote well-being.

Setting the stage for an exploration of strategies to navigate and thrive through various life changes.

Section 1: Understanding the Nature of Change

Discussing the nature of change and its impact on individuals and families.

Exploring common life changes, such as relocation, career transitions, and loss, and their effects on family dynamics.

Emphasizing the importance of embracing change as an opportunity for growth and adaptation.

Section 2: Building Resilience

Defining resilience and its role in navigating change and adversity.

Discussing the characteristics and skills associated with resilience.

Providing practical strategies for building resilience within the family unit.

Section 3: Communication and Support during Transitions

Emphasizing the importance of open and honest communication during times of change.

Discussing the role of empathy and active listening in providing support to family members.

Providing guidance on fostering a sense of togetherness and solidarity during transitions.

Section 4: Flexibility and Adaptability

Discussing the significance of flexibility and adaptability in navigating change.

Exploring strategies for cultivating a mindset of adaptability within the family.

Providing examples of how flexibility and adaptability can promote positive outcomes during times of change.

Section 5: Managing Stress and Emotions

Discussing the potential stress and emotional challenges that accompany change.

Providing practical techniques for managing stress and promoting emotional well-being during transitions.

Encouraging self-care practices and seeking support when needed.

Section 6: Finding Opportunities in Change

Shifting the perspective on change and exploring the potential opportunities it presents.

Discussing the importance of reframing challenges as growth opportunities.

Encouraging family members to embrace change as a chance for personal and collective development.

Conclusion:

Summarizing the key insights and takeaways from the chapter.

Emphasizing the transformative power of adaptability and resilience in navigating change within the family.

Inspiring readers to embrace change with openness, cultivate resilience, and support one another, creating a family environment that thrives through life's inevitable transitions.

Chapter 9: Making a Difference: Giving Back as a Family

Recognizing the importance of giving back to the community and making a positive impact as a family.

Exploring how engaging in philanthropy and acts of service can strengthen family bonds and foster empathy and compassion.

Setting the stage for an exploration of strategies to engage in meaningful giving back as a family.

Section 1: Understanding the Power of Giving Back

Discussing the impact of giving back on personal growth and family dynamics.

Exploring the benefits of instilling values of compassion, empathy, and social responsibility in family members.

Highlighting the transformative effects of acts of service on both the recipients and the givers.

Section 2: Identifying Causes and Passion Projects

Encouraging family members to explore their passions and identify causes they feel strongly about.

Discussing the importance of aligning philanthropic efforts with personal values and interests.

Providing guidance on researching and selecting reputable organizations and projects to support.

Section 3: Volunteering as a Family

Discussing the benefits of volunteering as a family.

Providing practical tips for finding volunteer opportunities that are suitable for all family members.

Emphasizing the value of shared experiences and the sense of purpose that comes from volunteering together.

Section 4: Philanthropic Giving

Discussing the various ways families can engage in philanthropy and charitable giving.

Exploring options such as financial donations, fundraising initiatives, and in-kind contributions.

Highlighting the importance of involving children in the decision-making process and explaining the impact of their giving.

Section 5: Acts of Kindness in Everyday Life

Discussing the significance of incorporating acts of kindness into everyday life.

Providing examples of simple gestures that can make a meaningful difference in the lives of others.

Encouraging family members to practice kindness, empathy, and generosity towards others on a regular basis.

Section 6: Cultivating a Culture of Giving Back

Discussing the importance of fostering a culture of giving back within the family.

Providing guidance on creating family traditions and rituals that center around acts of service.

Encouraging ongoing conversations about the impact of giving back and the value of collective action.

Conclusion:

Summarizing the key insights and takeaways from the chapter.

Emphasizing the transformative power of giving back as a family in creating a positive impact on the world.

Inspiring readers to actively engage in acts of service and philanthropy, fostering a culture of compassion, empathy, and making a difference in their communities and beyond.

Chapter 10: Overcoming Challenges Together

Recognizing that challenges are an inevitable part of life and can strengthen family bonds when faced together.

Exploring how overcoming challenges as a family builds resilience, fosters problem-solving skills, and promotes unity.

Setting the stage for an exploration of strategies to navigate and triumph over challenges as a cohesive family unit.

Section 1: Acknowledging and Accepting Challenges

Discussing the importance of acknowledging and accepting challenges as a normal part of life.

Emphasizing the value of reframing challenges as opportunities for growth and learning.

Encouraging open and honest communication within the family about the challenges being faced.

Section 2: Supporting Each Other Emotionally

Discussing the significance of emotional support during challenging times.

Providing guidance on active listening, empathy, and validation of emotions within the family.

Encouraging family members to offer comfort, encouragement, and understanding to one another.

Section 3: Developing Problem-Solving Skills

Emphasizing the importance of developing problem-solving skills as a family.

Providing strategies for fostering a collaborative problem-solving approach.

Encouraging brainstorming, creative thinking, and the exploration of multiple solutions.

Section 4: Building Resilience and Adaptability

Discussing the role of resilience and adaptability in overcoming challenges.

Exploring ways to cultivate resilience within the family unit.

Providing practical tips for adapting to change and bouncing back from setbacks.

Section 5: Seeking External Support

Discussing the benefits of seeking external support during challenging times.

Encouraging families to reach out to trusted friends, mentors, or professionals when needed.

Providing guidance on accessing community resources or professional help, if necessary.

Section 6: Finding Strength in Unity

Emphasizing the power of unity and togetherness in overcoming challenges.

Discussing the importance of fostering a sense of belonging and shared purpose within the family.

Encouraging family members to lean on one another for support and work together as a cohesive unit.

Conclusion:

Summarizing the key insights and takeaways from the chapter.

Emphasizing the transformative power of overcoming challenges together as a family.

Inspiring readers to face challenges head-on, fostering resilience, problem-solving skills, and a deepened sense of unity within their family, ultimately emerging stronger and more connected.

Chapter 11: Healing and Forgiveness: Restoring Family Bonds

Recognizing the significance of healing and forgiveness in repairing strained or broken family bonds.

Exploring how the processes of healing and forgiveness can promote healing, growth, and restoration within the family.

Setting the stage for an exploration of strategies to foster healing and forgiveness in order to restore family bonds.

Section 1: Understanding the Importance of Healing and Forgiveness

Discussing the impact of unresolved conflicts, hurt, and resentment on family relationships.

Exploring the transformative power of healing and forgiveness in promoting emotional well-being and harmony.

Emphasizing the role of empathy, compassion, and self-reflection in the healing and forgiveness process.

Section 2: Acknowledging and Addressing Past Wounds

Discussing the importance of acknowledging and addressing past wounds within the family.

Encouraging open and honest communication about the pain and hurt that may have occurred.

Providing guidance on creating a safe and supportive environment for sharing and understanding each other's perspectives.

Section 3: Cultivating Empathy and Understanding

Emphasizing the importance of empathy and understanding in the healing and forgiveness process.

Encouraging family members to actively listen, seek to understand, and validate each other's feelings and experiences.

Providing strategies for fostering empathy and compassion within the family.

Section 4: Practicing Self-Reflection and Personal Growth

Discussing the role of self-reflection and personal growth in the healing and forgiveness journey.

Encouraging family members to examine their own behaviors, beliefs, and contributions to conflicts.

Providing guidance on embracing personal growth, accountability, and taking steps towards positive change.

Section 5: Nurturing Trust and Rebuilding Relationships

Discussing the process of rebuilding trust within the family.

Providing strategies for creating a foundation of trust through consistent communication, reliability, and honesty.

Encouraging patience and understanding as relationships are gradually restored.

Section 6: The Power of Forgiveness

Exploring the transformative power of forgiveness in healing and restoring family bonds.

Discussing the misconceptions about forgiveness and its connection to reconciliation.

Providing guidance on the forgiveness process and how to cultivate forgiveness within the family.

Section 7: Establishing Healthy Boundaries

Discussing the importance of establishing and respecting healthy boundaries within the family.

Providing strategies for setting boundaries that promote self-care, respect, and emotional well-being.

Emphasizing the role of boundaries in maintaining healthy and harmonious family dynamics.

Conclusion:

Summarizing the key insights and takeaways from the chapter.

Emphasizing the transformative power of healing and forgiveness in restoring family bonds.

Inspiring readers to embark on a journey of healing, empathy, and forgiveness, fostering a renewed sense of connection, harmony, and love within their family.

Chapter 12: Passing on the Torch: Ensuring a Lasting Legacy

Recognizing the importance of creating and passing on a meaningful family legacy.

Exploring how intentionally shaping and preserving a legacy can strengthen family bonds and provide a sense of purpose and continuity.

Setting the stage for an exploration of strategies to ensure a lasting legacy for future generations.

Section 1: Reflecting on Values and Beliefs

Encouraging family members to reflect on their shared values, beliefs, and traditions.

Discussing the significance of identifying core principles that define the family's identity and guiding principles.

Providing guidance on engaging in meaningful conversations to clarify and solidify the family's values and beliefs.

Section 2: Documenting Family History and Stories

Emphasizing the importance of preserving and sharing family history and stories.

Discussing the benefits of documenting memories, experiences, and lessons learned.

Providing practical tips for collecting and organizing family photos, documents, and oral histories.

Section 3: Intergenerational Connections and Mentorship

Discussing the value of fostering intergenerational connections within the family.

Encouraging mentorship and guidance from older family members to younger generations.

Providing strategies for creating opportunities for meaningful interactions and knowledge transfer.

Section 4: Passing on Skills, Knowledge, and Traditions

Discussing the importance of passing on practical skills, knowledge, and traditions.

Exploring ways to teach and share family traditions, cultural practices, and specialized skills.

Encouraging hands-on learning experiences and shared activities that promote the transfer of knowledge.

Section 5: Philanthropy and Social Responsibility

Discussing the role of philanthropy and social responsibility in the family legacy.

Exploring opportunities for engaging in charitable giving and community service as a family.

Emphasizing the importance of instilling a sense of social responsibility in future generations.

Section 6: Creating a Family Mission Statement

Discussing the benefits of creating a family mission statement.

Providing guidance on collaboratively developing a mission statement that reflects the family's values, goals, and aspirations.

Emphasizing the importance of revisiting and revising the mission statement over time.

Section 7: Celebrating Milestones and Family Rituals

Discussing the significance of celebrating family milestones and establishing meaningful rituals.

Providing suggestions for creating traditions and rituals that strengthen family bonds and mark important moments.

Encouraging the active participation of all family members in the creation and maintenance of these traditions.

Conclusion:

Summarizing the key insights and takeaways from the chapter.

Emphasizing the importance of intentionally shaping and passing on a lasting family legacy.

Inspiring readers to engage in purposeful actions that ensure the preservation of values, traditions, and a sense of identity, allowing their family legacy to endure for generations to come.

www.ingramcontent.com/pod-product-compliance
Lightning Source LLC
Chambersburg PA
CBHW070342120526
44590CB00017B/2989